A Bite-Sized Public A

GW00391629

The Case for Brexit

Edited by
John Mair, Alex De Ruyter and Neil Fowler

Published by Bite-Sized Books Ltd 2019

Bite-Sized Books Ltd Cleeve Croft, Cleeve Road, Goring RG8 9BJ UK
information@bite-sizedbooks.com
Registered in the UK. Company Registration No: 9395379

Bite-Sized Books Ltd Cleeve Croft, Cleeve Road, Goring RG8 9BJ UK
information@bite-sizedbooks.com
Registered in the UK. Company Registration No: 9395379
ISBN: 9781794216907

Acknowledgements

These 'hackademic' books are always team efforts. John Mair conceived this as a counter intuitive contribution to the Brexit debate. It was brought to reality by his co-editors Neil Fowler and Alex De Ruyter. Paul Davies is the ideal publisher for these volumes.

Most of all though we need to thank the authors.

None are paid, nor the editors too. They gave willingly and against a very tight deadline. To them – and to Sir John Redwood for his foreword – we are very grateful.

We hope the book stimulates.

John Mair, Oxford

Alex De Ruyter Birmingham

Neil Fowler, Northumberland

The Editors

John Mair has taught journalism at the Universities of Coventry, Kent, Northampton, Brunel, Edinburgh Napier, Guyana and the Communication University of China. He has edited 26 'hackademic' volumes over the last eight years on subjects ranging from trust in television, the health of investigative journalism, reporting the 'Arab Spring', to three volumes on the Leveson Inquiry. John also created the Coventry Conversations, which attracted 350 media movers and shakers to Coventry University. Since then, he has launched the Northampton Chronicles, Media Mondays at Napier and most recently the Harrow Conversations at Westminster University. In a previous life, he was an award-winning producer/director for the BBC, ITV and Channel 4, and a secondary school teacher.

Neil Fowler has been in journalism since graduation, starting life as trainee reporter on the *Leicester Mercury*. He went on to edit four regional dailies, including *The Journal* in the north east of England and *The Western Mail* in Wales. He was then publisher of *The Toronto Sun* in Canada before returning to the UK to edit *Which?* magazine. In 2010/11 he was the Guardian Research Fellow at Oxford University's Nuffield College where he investigated the decline and future of regional and local newspapers in the UK. He remains an Associate Member of Nuffield and now acts as an adviser to organisations on their management and their external and internal communications and media policies and strategies.

Alex de Ruyter is a professor at Birmingham City University and serves as Director of its Centre for Brexit Studies. He brings a wealth of research experience and academic engagement in the areas of globalisation, regional economic development, labour market and social exclusion issues. He has published more than 60 academic outputs in leading national and international economic journals and has been the recipient of research funding, including being an investigator in an ESRC funded study on the effects on subsequent employment experience of workers from MG Rover after plant closure in 2005.

Professor de Ruyter has undertaken numerous media interviews and is currently researching on the likely impact of Brexit on the UK automotive supply chain in addition to exploring working in the 'gig economy'. He is also a Board member of the Regional Studies Association.

Contents

Foreword

Still true in 2018 as it was in 2016

Sir John Redwood MP

The People's vote in 2016 decided we will leave the EU. That was a good decision, taken to restore democratic control over our laws, our money and our borders. It is Parliament's job as promised to implement it promptly and well. There is no need for a second vote, which would sow confusion and anger the Leave-voting majority.

The big gain from Brexit as the economic contributions to this book make clear will come from spending our own money on our own priorities, and from pursuing a UK economic and business policy which is best for us.

As 2019 dawns two of the news items remind us of the damaging impact the EU can have on our economy. The new fishing policy may have got rid of the unacceptable discarding of dead fish but leaves fishing businesses in the UK with the threat of having to cease fishing and trading as soon as a quota for a particular fish is hit. A small fishing boat may be beached for a long period if it happens to catch a few fish of a species it was not targeting.

An ECJ judgement has found the payments the UK makes to ensure there is capacity available in our electricity system are illegal, leaving us in doubt about how we guarantee to keep the lights on under the very expensive and regulated approach laid down by the EU. Rebuilding our fishing industry and putting some common sense into our power system can be wins from Brexit.

Is Mrs May's withdrawal agreement acceptable?

The draft Withdrawal Agreement is an unacceptable surrender of UK sovereignty and money. It is the opposite of Brexit, planning to lock us into EU rules and budget requirements for another 21 months minimum and maybe for another 45 months. This time period would be used in talks about a future partnership and trading arrangements.

Given the failure of the EU to come up with proposals on the future over the 30 months of futile negotiations so far, it is difficult to see how the next set of talks will be more productive, especially given the way the Withdrawal Agreement undermines the UK bargaining position. If we sign up to giving the EU most of what they want in advance of the new talks, why should they make a better offer than they have so far?

Why did we vote to leave?

We voted for Brexit to change our relationship with the EU to one of friendship and mutual collaboration where it makes sense to do so. We want to be free to make our own trade deals with the rest of the world where we conduct a majority of our trade and where the trade grows more quickly than with the EU.

We want to rebuild our fishing industry after years of depredations? under the Common Fishing Policy. We want to grow more food at home and cut the food miles, after years of rising dependence on EU sources under the Common Agricultural Policy. We want to settle our own regulatory regime for everything from digital to media, in a way which promotes innovation and business success.

The new dawn?

Once we leave the EU the first task should be to provide a welcome boost to our public services out of the money we have saved. Not signing the withdrawal agreement frees more than £39bn of cash otherwise committed to the EU. We owe them nothing once we have left.

Let us hire more nurses and doctors, teachers and security forces, and invest in better transport. We should also use some of the money for tax cuts so there is a Brexit bonus for every household in the land.

We could take VAT from domestic heating fuel and remove it from green products, something we are not allowed to do as members of the EU. We should also abate Vehicle Excise Duty to help our car industry, which has been badly damaged by recent tax and regulatory policies and cut Stamp Duties to let more people buy and own the home of their choice.

If we use the freedoms and the money we save sensibly there will be a boost to incomes and output in our economy. The UK can once again be a leader for free trade globally, and a force for good in the world as we regain our vote and voice in international bodies where the EU currently pre-empts our role.

Reasons to leave in 2018

The case for Brexit was good in 2016. It is even better today, as we see the EU wedded to austerity policies for the member states and ploughing on with regulations that get in the way of more jobs and innovation. Let's take back control. Let's do so on 29 March 2019. Let's be optimistic about a future which will then rest in our own hands.

The biggest gain from Brexit is to restore our independence and our democracy. Important decisions will be taken in the UK by a government we vote for, and by a government we can dismiss if it lets us down.

About the contributor

The Rt Hon Sir John Redwood is the Conservative MP for Wokingham, He was formerly Secretary of State for Wales in John Major's Cabinet, and was twice an unsuccessful challenger for the leadership of the Conservative Party in the 1990s. He headed up Margaret Thatcher's Policy Unit and has been a Brexiteer for three decades. He was knighted in the 2019 New Year's Honours list.

Introduction

The academic Brexiteers have a voice

John Mair and Alex De Ruyter

This is a unique volume. As the UK prepares to Brexit – softish or hard – on 29 March 2019, it gives a platform to the academic Brexiteers – the ABs – those who provide the intellectual firepower for the louder up-front politicians like Boris Johnson and David Davis.

The ABs are the provisional thinking arm of Britain's Brexit army. They were the fringe for many decades, today they are the mainstream – 17.4m voters put them there on 23 June 2016 in the Great Referendum.

They are economists (many 'free traders' like Patrick Minford and David Paton), historians like Robert Tombs, and those who 'jumped ship' like John Mills of Labour Leave. The years in the intellectual wilderness has taken its toll. Much of their scholarship comes from within a 'Brexit Bubble' of the like-minded. If they disagree with the results of a particular economic model they invent their own. Their arguments are not always that easy to follow or indeed to swallow. We leave the reader to judge their worth.

The grandfather of the political Brexiteers is the (newly ennobled) Sir John Redwood MP. He is a serial Eurosceptic and has been one for decades. His voice has always been prominent in the case against the EU. He headed Margaret Thatcher's Policy Unit and later served as Welsh Secretary in her Cabinet. That did not stop her successor John Major labelling him one of the Tory Eurosceptic 'bastards' in 1993.

In his foreword , specially written for this book, *'Still true in 2018 as it was in 2016'* Sir John lauds the result as "a good decision, taken to restore democratic control over our laws, our money and our borders. It is Parliament's job as promised to implement it promptly and well".

Events since have confirmed him in his hard-line view. "Given the failure of the EU to come up with proposals on the future over the 30 months of futile negotiations so far, it is difficult to see how the next set of talks will be more productive, especially given the way the withdrawal agreement undermines the UK bargaining position." The choice is as it ever was: "Let's take back control. Let's do so on 29 March 2019. Let's be optimistic about a future which will then rest in our own hands". No doubts there then.

Sir Andrew Wood, a career diplomat – latterly as the Ambassador to Russia (a prime Foreign Office posting) is more nuanced in his view, as one would expect of one with that metier.

In *'Is the UK stuck to the EU Tar Baby?'* he uses the tar baby metaphor of Joel Chandler Harris's 1904 fable to put it in context. In modern usage, *tar baby* refers to a problem situation that is only aggravated by additional involvement with it.

He concludes that: "The EU is not now a safe or comfortable haven for the UK. Britain needs to decide on new priorities in the event of its choosing to restore its independent authority by the only option now apparently available to it, leaving on WTO terms", and calls for a 'clear decision' for Britain to 'restore its' international reputation'.

John Mills is an outlier amongst this (fairly) Conservative company. He is a former Labour Councillor who chaired Labour Leave, which played some part in getting Labour voters across the 'Leave' line.

In *'A second referendum'* he looks at the arguments to be had if a 'People's Vote' occurs before the UK leaves the EU. Mills is not convinced the result would be much different to the first as the 'fundamentals' are the same, but calls for a firm steer from the politicians to the people "What we need more than anything else is a settlement which gives enough people sufficient comfort for there to be a permanent relationship between the UK and the EU for the future, which most people accept," he writes.

Robert Tombs is Professor of French History at Cambridge. That does not prevent him being anti-EU, which he sees as a de-stabilising force across the Continent.

In *'Brexit: once desirable, now indispensable'* he says the 2016 vote was 'prudent' then but in 2019 is vital as 'a clear and unambiguous' Brexit has become necessary to resolve the issue with minimum political damage now and in the future. An ambiguous or duplicitous outcome would certainly perpetuate our present discontents. If a clear and legal popular vote were actually to be overridden or reversed, unknown dangers for our national cohesion and democratic legitimacy would be created, he believes.

So to the Economists for Brexit. They are a club with not many members. Professor David Paton of Nottingham University is firmly one.

He says in *'Why economists can and should disagree about everything ...including Brexit'* that the false (in his view) negative consensus of 'expert economists' on the results of leaving needs to be broken; time to look to the positive such as the possibility of increased FDI (Foreign Direct Investment) in post-Brexit Britain, *'...for example if multinationals think it important to make sure they have a foothold in the strategically important UK market when our ties with the EU are loosened'*.

But he does admit the empirical evidence on this is mixed...

Fellow 'EFB' club members Graham Gudgin and Ken Coutts, both associated with Cambridge University, rub in the false forecasts made by the Remain camp in 2016.

In *'How the economics profession got it wrong on Brexit,'* they point out that the mainstream forecasters were wrong on the 2008 banking crisis and even more wrong in 2016. Chancellor George Osborne and HM Treasury simply miscalculated by accident or design or using the wrong models.

They say: "The short-term forecasts published during the referendum campaign, were clearly overly-pessimistic and a replication of long-term forecasts reveal important flaws which exaggerate pessimism". The obvious failure of the short-term forecasts made in 2016 have weakened the already faltering public confidence in official forecasts, they say, but the strongly partisan nature of the Brexit debate means that official predictions are still called in aid of the case against Brexit despite the poor record on the short-term forecasts.

The guru of the EFB club is Professor Patrick Minford, now at Cardiff University, but latterly at Liverpool. He is the academic equivalent of John Redwood – a serial Eurosceptic and at some points almost the only academic economist making the case for Brexit. His chickens will come home to roost in March and he is cock-a-hoop. His solution very simple. Britain should Crash out and take WTO conditions Go Back to the Future!

In his chapter *'The default option of a World Trade Deal is the best available'* he says it is time to recognise that we are headed towards the default option of no deal, or more accurately, an exit under WTO rules, better called a 'World Trade Deal' and adds: "Leaving the EU cleanly allows us to move our policies to free trade, and good regulation, regaining our economic sovereignty. In all our history these policies have served us well. and they will do so again today".

And, finally, Research Professor Emeritus Gwythian Prins of the London School of Economics. Like Sir John Redwood, he asserts in *'The case for Brexit in December 2018'* that the two long-standing arguments are even stronger now than they were two years ago. But with Robert Tombs, he also believes that the conduct of the irreconcilable remainers means that the original two arguments have been joined by a new one; and that this new danger, he believes, contains an unprecedented threat – to our national security.

"The (May) 'deal' surrenders British national security by subordinating UK defence forces to Military EU control and compromising UK Intelligence capabilities. It puts at risk the fundamental Anglosphere alliances, specifically the vital Five Eyes Alliance and thereby threatens western security", he says.

Chapter 1

Is the UK stuck to the EU Tar Baby?[1]

The exhausting introspection of the last two and half years has brought us back to the question posed in June 2016: should the UK stay in or stay dependent on the EU, or should it regain its sovereignty? The EU is not now a safe or comfortable haven for the UK. Britain needs to decide on new priorities in the event of its choosing to restore its independent authority by the only option now apparently available to it, leaving on WTO terms. Andrew Wood says why this is the case

The 2016 Referendum posed a clear choice before the British public: should the UK leave the European Union, including the single market, the customs union, and the jurisdiction of the European Court of Justice, or not? By the end of 2018 the intensity of barely structured democratic debate, exacerbated by uncertain leadership in both the main political parties, as well the Scottish National Party's focus on resuscitating the cause of Scotland's independence, had obscured the public's fully recorded answer to this basic question.

Electors were later said however to have been misled, and not to have been able to give an informed and definitive verdict. The choices before them in the run up to 29 March 2019 were by the end of 2018 in practice reduced to accepting the EU's terms as imposed on Prime Minister May, agreeing to a referendum intended to help them to revisit and revise their 2016 choice, or 'crashing out' on WTO rules.

The international view

President Trump was concise and accurate when he remarked to reporters outside The White House on 26 November 2018 that the EU had secured a great deal, by implication at the UK's expense, in its withdrawal negotiations with Mrs May. He added that it could make future trade with the USA more difficult. Other foreign leaders were more tactful but appeared to share his assessment.

If Parliament had on 15 January accepted the terms of the withdrawal agreement endorsed by the EU, and by Mrs May, or if it were to accept a somewhat adapted version of it in the future, that agreement would be legally binding and would as such impose strict conditions on subsequent negotiations covering future trading arrangements between the UK and the EU. There would certainly be two years or more of damaging dispute to come within the UK, and between the UK and the EU, in that event. EU negotiators would be at critical advantage in the contest. The record suggests that they would use it without hesitation.

Has the UK lost international respect?

The UK's international authority has been compromised over the past two years. The 2016 Referendum vote was widely taken abroad as being populist, paralleled with the election of Donald Trump that year to be President of the USA. It was regularly held to be a retreat from the world, not an effort to reshape Britain's position in it. Reports of racist or nationalist elements within the British public were quite widely believed, at least at first .

The apparent inability of the Government in London to follow a coherent and consistent policy or to impose its own agenda on Brussels, or even to maintain some sort of order within its own ranks has seemed to many both abroad and at home to illustrate an enfeeblement of the UK as a whole. The Prime Minister's failure to make good in the 2017 General Election parliamentary elections, coupled with the picture of her as a lowly regarded and sometimes mocked supplicant in Brussels have reinforced that impression.

Four British weaknesses

Four other factors have weakened Britain.

The first is the predictable volume of domestic criticism, a fair amount of it alarmist in tone, and some of it with what appears to be the endorsement of the government itself. Talking ourselves down is an endemic fault of modern Britain.

Second is the absence of evident examination, let alone clear planning, as to what policies are to be considered once the UK has left the EU. Vague references to 'new trade deals' or to 'becoming a global country', whatever that means, are not enough to persuade the outside world or the British public for that matter of what the UK's considered long-term purposes in pursuing Brexit might be.

Third, there is the Conservative government's apparent fear of losing the next election to Jeremy Corbyn's Labour Party.

The present UK government ought to be consoled and emboldened by the evident facts that the Labour opposition has no coherent or persuasive policies to offer on managing Britain's future relationship with the EU, and that some at least of the proposals Labour has in mind if it manages to win a future election are deeply troubling for foreign as well as domestic investors. The UK's economic and social performance, including by comparison with that of the EU as a whole or that of its more successful members, is much better than is generally supposed.[2]

But, factor four, too much in and about the UK is seen and acted upon through the Brexit lens.

The assured rigidity of the EU

The EU, by contrast, has seen or at least affected to see Brexit as the least of its problems. The French for example have argued that the UK has demanded to leave the Union, and that the UK should deal with the consequences without expecting the EU to change in response. There is a crude negotiating logic to that. But it fails to take into account what to the British would seem to be the wider interest of a mutually beneficial future relationship with the UK once it has left the Union.

The UK will after all whatever happens then still be part of Europe, with common economic, security, political and cultural interests to share with those remaining in the EU, as well as those who have never been members of it.

But the EU is in the first place a political undertaking, whose chief actors prize their project of preserving and developing ever closer political union above their immediate economic interests, at least in the sense that they suppose the latter are dependent on enhancing the former. The British have never entirely accepted that either for themselves or in recognising the force that it exerts within the EU itself.

The structure of the EU is nevertheless such as to dictate its central attitudes: the Commissioners are national appointees in essence answerable to themselves as a group, not independent political actors answerable to national or institutional EU democratic control; and the central motor of the Union as a whole is acknowledged to be France and Germany. British attempts to improve this construction in the name of protecting or enhancing the differing circumstances of member states have not been effective. 'Subsidiarity' has generally lost out to the forces of centralisation and the consequent distortions inherent in an effort to establish one rule for all within the EU.

Three EU weaknesses

Negotiations under any withdrawal deal that might eventually follow British and EU formal agreement to its terms would be dictated by the constraints that the UK would have accepted in the knowledge that circumstances within the EU will evolve, 'not necessarily to our advantage'.[3]

If the UK decides to remain within the EU after all, which many within the Union as well as the UK hope it may, it also follows that the UK will be bound by the way that the EU will have proceeded in the interim. London would do well to take into account, too, weaknesses that the EU now confronts before deciding on either option. Brexit is among other things an expression of a wider set of related issues that confront EU decision makers.

First, the Euro has not been the success it was imagined that it would be on its creation in stimulating growth and spreading prosperity among its members. It has, on the contrary, harmed some member states while benefitting others. It is not clear that those states under the obligation to adopt the Euro in due course will in practice do so. The measures forced upon Eurozone states in difficulty following the global economic crisis that began in 2008 were questionable in their wisdom. The Eurozone has yet to establish effective central supranational mechanisms that would enable it to deal with a future global crisis, despite fears that one may be in prospect. But the Euro is an essential tool for the pursuit of ever closer unity and dismantling it would be difficult.

Second, migration. There are ironies in the UK being accused of prejudice against free movement of labour despite the fact that it opened its doors before nearly all its partners to people from those countries that had just joined the EU, but the ideological case for free movement in the EU is nonetheless a strong one. The practical difficulties in dealing with immigration into the Union and their consequences for free movement within the EU are nonetheless both difficult and contentious - as well as unsolved so far.

Third, the relationship between the member states of the EU and its directing organs is unbalanced, and disputed. The question of where sovereignty lies was crucial to the British vote in 2016. Other member states, the latest being Italy, contest the right of Brussels based organs to issue directives overriding the decisions of democratically ruled EU states. Those organs encompass a set of ideas that carry force, along with its logic of promoting unified action across a wide range of fields. But they lack the legitimacy needed to secure their execution. Despite some of the aspirational rhetoric, there is no appetite within the EU to address this fundamental problem.

The future?

The rejection by Parliament on 15 January of the deal agreed between the British Prime Minister of the day and the EU has faced the UK with a stark return to the question posed in 2016: stay or go? That question would remain at the heart of the matter even in the improbable event of some adjustments being accepted by the EU that would allow a future variant of the present text to be accepted by Parliament after all, and negotiations on eventual trade regulations under its terms were to begin.

There are those in Parliament and beyond it who appear desperate to evade answering the conundrum as to whether the UK would be wiser in present circumstances to remain part of a supra-national organisation, perhaps covered by some new cloak of Norwegian or other design if a reversion to full membership of the European Union is not practicable, or to make a clear break for independent sovereign status now. Where one thinks the EU may be headed in the future in either case is of critical importance.

So too is the confidence one may or may not have in the UK being able to manage its own affairs and to make its own choices in the years to come. The way that EU negotiators have tried to bind their UK opposite numbers into existing arrangements under the deal on offer suggests that they may fear Britain could do it disturbingly well.

A clear decision now would help the UK to address problems beyond its relationship with the rest of the EU and restore its international reputation. The proposition that a 'no-deal' exit should legally be ruled out would if accepted in effect be to rule that the UK should remain in the European Union. The EU has after all insisted that what it has agreed to is the only option it will accept. Parliament has rejected it. If one seriously believes that the EU and its individual members would revenge themselves on the UK for daring to leave on WTO terms to the extent that some have suggested, would it be right to remain in such an organisation after all?

Notes

1.   The Tar Baby

Br'er Rabbit and the Tar-Baby, drawing by E.W. Kemble from The Tar-Baby, by Joel Chandler Harris, 1904

The Tar-Baby is a doll, featured in a classic children's story, made of tar and turpentine used by the villainous Br'er Fox to entrap Br'er

Rabbit. The more that Br'er Rabbit fights the Tar-Baby, the more entangled he becomes. In modern usage, *tar baby* refers to a problem situation that is only aggravated by additional involvement with it.

(An explanation derived from Wikipedia)

2. Fraser Nelson's Comment article in the *Daily Telegraph* of 28 December 2018 headed "Despite the Brexit warnings, Britain has never been a better place to live" is a lively justification, among many others, of the UK's success independent of the country's membership to date of the European Union. His account is drawn from news articles built up over the last couple of years which included the words "despite Brexit" (relevant or not). His argument that they painted a picture of an extraordinary country has considerable force.
3. As the Japanese Emperor put it in 1945.

About the contributor

Sir Andrew Wood was a member of the British Diplomatic Service between 1961 and 2000. Three periods in Moscow (as Ambassador 1995-2000) and two in Belgrade (as Ambassador 1985-1989) gave lessons in the fragility of federal structures, as did two postings to Washington, where the US Civil War has not been forgotten. He has acted on behalf of a number of commercial organisations with interests in Russia and other former Soviet countries following his retirement from the FCO, and has been an Associate Fellow with the Russia and Eurasia Programme at Chatham House over the past decade.

Chapter 2

A second referendum?

John Mills considers what the Leave arguments might be if there is second referendum pre-Brexit

There probably will not be a 'People's Vote' or second referendum – despite all the efforts there have been by some people to promote one. Getting it to happen requires primary legislation for which the current Conservative government is unlikely to want to make time. Even if parliamentary votes force it to do so, there may not be a majority in Parliament to get a bill through, authorising a referendum to take place.

In addition, for this to happen, Article 50 would have to be extended, to enable the UK to stay in the EU until the Referendum was held, otherwise it would be about applying to re-join instead of staying in.

Extending Article 50 may not be easy as it requires all the EU 27 states and the Commission and European Parliament to agree to it being done, quite possibly with concessions being required in return. Then, what would the questions be? How much damage would be done by a further long period of uncertainty and division? How much bitterness would another referendum stir up? Would the outcome be what the proponents very largely want – a decision that the UK should stay with the EU – or would the result be the same as last time?

All these problems mean that a second referendum will probably never happen – but in these uncertain times anything is possible, which makes it worth considering what the arguments might be on the Leave side if a People's Vote does materialise.

Referendum re-run – what should Leave say?

First, there is the key democratic issue. During the run-up to the June 2016 Referendum, solemn assurances were made by the Government and many others that that the outcome of the vote would be respected, and that Parliament would implement the result of the Referendum, whatever it was. The Referendum was not to be advisory; it was to be decisive. This was reinforced at the time of the General Election in June 2017, when both the Conservative and Labour Parties – who, between them, accounted for more than 80 per cent of all the MPs then elected – included in their manifestos promises to implement Brexit.

The triggering of Article 50 by a huge Parliamentary majority in March 2017 was another example of widespread acceptance of the decisiveness of the June 2016 EU vote. For this now to be called in question – reflecting a well-established EU routine where referendum results which the EU does not like, trigger off new referendums until the 'right' answer is given – is likely to go down extremely badly with a large section of the UK electorate, who were well aware that leaving the UK was not going to be an easy ride in the best of circumstances and who were quite willing – if I came to it – to pay an economic price for greater control over their futures.

Re-run – the practical arguments

Then there are all the practical arguments and factors which persuaded many Leave people to vote the way they did in June 2016. These include the size of our net annual payment to the EU, which has regularly been in excess of £10bn a year; the widespread desire for the UK to have control of our borders and who is allowed to live and work here; and a determination to have the laws by which we live in the hands of our own parliament rather than by unaccountable people abroad.

We wanted then – and want now – to see the UK out of both the Common Agricultural and the Common Fisheries Policies, neither of which have been remotely in the interest of the British people. We also wish to be able to enter into free trade deals with the parts of the world which are growing much more rapidly than the EU, instead of being blocked from doing so by our membership of the EU Customs Union.

To achieve these objectives, we would have to leave both the Single Market and the EU Customs Union as well as the EU itself. This would steer the UK clear of the integrationist proposals widely shared among the EU elite but never supported by all but a very small minority in the UK.

If the Eurozone is to survive, it is clear that it can only do so by establishing a banking and then a political union on a scale which polls show that the vast majority of the people in the UK have never supported. With the example of Greece in mind, in particular, there would be substantial advantages to the UK of being outside the EU if the Eurozone fractures and fragments, as may well happen.

Re-run – the emotions

While these points of view underpinned the economic and political cases for Leave, there is no doubt that emotion as well as practicality played a large part in the June 2016 vote and that it would do so again if there was another referendum. In particular, there was a huge appeal behind the slogan of 'Taking Back Control'.

As research has shown, very large numbers of people thought that their lives were largely controlled and shaped by people who had little time or respect for them, who were not interested in their fears and concerns, and who were far too remote and unaccountable.

The EU Referendum was certainly about the EU itself as an example of the kind of remoteness which so many people resented. It also, however, became a general opportunity for large numbers of people, many of whom had not voted for a long time, to vent their frustration at the way governance generally had been managed in the UK. This phenomenon would very probably recur.

Bored of Brexit?

Would sentiments of this kind be strong enough to overcome the feeling among some people that they had had enough of Brexit and just wanted to sink back, by staying in the EU, into less tormented times when radio, television and the newspapers were not filled day after day with the problems caused by the way Brexit was being handled?

Perhaps, but these will be very probably be offset by those who feel that the EU 27 have behaved extremely harshly with the UK over Brexit and who do not like being told what to do in the way which we have experienced over the last couple of years.

There will also be plenty of people who resent having a second referendum foisted upon them after the electorate had given a clear decision first time round. Didn't our political class get the message, they will think, when 17.4m people voted for Leave in the biggest single democratic exercise the country has ever undertaken? The result may well be determination to tell them the same thing again.

Re-run – too close to call?

All these factors suggest that another referendum would be a close call. Of course, the outcome would depend to a considerable extent on the way choices were presented to the electorate, and it is far from clear how this would be done.

If, as some have suggested, the choice was to be just between the deeply unsatisfactory Withdrawal Agreement and staying in, all the many people who would like to see the EU right out of the UK's political structures would be outraged that their preferred option had been excluded.

If a full exit is included, however, the balloting becomes much more complicated. What we do know is that relatively few people have changed their views on Brexit since June 2016. Recent polls have indicated an average of about 48 per cent in favour of Leave and 52 per cent Remain, but this is what the polls were telling us as the EU Referendum took place in 2016. The actual result, however, was the other way around, with 52 per cent against and 48 per cent for Leave. The same could easily happen again.

In conclusion

The reality is that not much has changed to the fundamentals since 2016 and Europe is as divisive both within and between our political parties as it has ever been.

What we need more than anything else is a settlement which gives enough people sufficient comfort for there to be a permanent relationship between the UK and the EU for the future, which most people accept.

Perhaps the strongest argument of all for Leave is that the UK staying in the EU will never do this but leaving the EU on close but independent terms with a comprehensive free-trade deal while retaining all the ways in which it makes sense for us to co-operate with our close continental neighbours, might do so. An outcome like this would not only satisfy nearly all Leavers, it could also provide Remainers with most of what they cherish most dearly.

A deal broadly along these lines was offered to us during 2018 by both Donald Tusk, the President of the European Council, and by Michel Barnier, the EU27's chief Brexit negotiator. Getting it into place should not be that difficult, especially as the starting position is complete regulatory alignment between the UK. Is it really too late for the UK to regroup and to fight hard for the kind of close but inter-governmental relationship – as opposed to being part of an integrationist political project – which most people in the UK would really like?

About the contributor

John Mills is an entrepreneur and economist who has long been involved with political matters. He was Chair of Labour Leave during the 2016 referendum campaign and he is founder of the think tank Labour Future. He is Chairman of John Mills Limited (JML) which specialises in selling high volume consumer products using audio-visual methods of promoting their sale. His main interests as an economist are the relatively poor performance of western economies compared with those in the East and the UK's relationship with the EU.

Chapter 3

Brexit: once desirable, now indispensable

The EU is destabilising politics across Europe. To vote to leave in 2016 was prudent. Now Brexit has become necessary for our own political legitimacy and to leave open the possibility for other countries to make a similar democratic choice, argues Robert Tombs

There are many reasons for the United Kingdom to leave the European Union. It is economically disadvantageous, most obviously in making permanent a huge balance of trade deficit, for which privilege we pay a substantial financial contribution.

It imposes regulations on economic activity which are arguably damaging and likely to increase. It strains our social and economic fabric by institutionalizing a large and uncontrolled influx of people.

But in my opinion, the most urgent reasons for withdrawing from the Union are political, and they fall into three broad categories: the EU's future ambitions; the destabilising effects of its policies across Europe; and the effects of the Brexit debate for our own political stability.

The EU's ambitions

As everyone knows, the European 'project' has always had as one of its basic aims the 'ever closer union' of the peoples of Europe. This might seem unexceptionable, but the means by which it has been pursued have always put top-down institutional action first, with popular consent assumed eventually to follow.

The context for this ambition goes back directly to the post-1945 period, but has its roots in the 1920s and before. Two world wars, it was argued, made some sort of European federation indispensable. The logic was that the world wars had been a consequence of national conflicts and of the extremism to which the peoples of Europe (or some of them) had succumbed. 'Populism' (as many now call it) was dangerous and had to be restrained and eventually neutered. The controlling economic levers – which in the 1950s were coal and steel – had to be put under international authority to prevent any nation (which really meant Germany) from being dangerous again.

This was, however, a dubious historical analysis. The two world wars had not been caused by populist extremism, but by authoritarian and expansionist regimes risking or deliberately seeking conflict. Popular patriotism had proved the most effective barrier against totalitarianism. Democracy was and is the best bulwark against war, and as long as European states remain democracies, war between them is unthinkable. But the European project has always treated democracy – that is, genuine popular choice – as a problem to be circumvented, as has been seen most recently in Greece, Italy, Catalonia and the United Kingdom whose perfectly legal choice to leave the EU has been treated as an attack to be resisted, even punished.

I think of this as the 'vanguard myth': an enlightened minority leads the way towards European unity, and the masses sooner or later accept the choices of their leaders as inevitable. President Emmanuel Macron is the latest exponent of such a view, expressed in an important speech at the Sorbonne on 26 September 2017. This method has undoubtedly been effective: European federalists have largely shaped the parameters and language of the debate into one of progressive 'Europeanism' versus reactionary 'populism'. Even in a country such as Greece, which has suffered so obviously from EU financial policies, the idea of actually leaving the EU inspires dread – dread of economic catastrophe and political chaos.

The EU is not content with controlling the intellectual debate. It backs up its arguments with both threats and inducements, as can be seen at present (January 2019) in its tense negotiations with the Italian government over budgetary restrictions. Ironically, the more damaging EU financial policies are, the greater the sense of vulnerability created in member states that try to oppose them. In the case of both Greece and Italy (and in several other states), the economic damage inflicted by the Eurozone and its austerity policies makes it seem more difficult and dangerous to resist or abandon them.

The Euro is the greatest symbol and embodiment of the ambitions of the EU so far attained: it was decided on by the most powerful member states (excepting Britain) despite many warnings of the dangers, all of which have been fulfilled or exceeded (Mody, 2018). But the need now to prevent a financial and economic disaster leads to calls for greater efforts to impose central control over the economic, financial, fiscal, welfare, defence, security and migration policies of the member states.

It is sometimes argued that these problems did not primarily affect Britain, which was not in the Eurozone and had various other opt-outs, and therefore that Britain had no compelling reasons for leaving the EU.

The argument of course goes both ways: what are the compelling reasons for staying in a failing organisation of which we were only partial members? Why wish to share responsibility for policies which are damaging to others and to ourselves, and which Britain often argued against? The facile answer that we should stay in to reform the system is nullified by the absence of any reform programme, other than increasing centralisation of the Eurozone, which we would in any case not be part of or willing to join.

Destabilising political effects

Not all the ills presently affecting the democratic world can be blamed on the EU – far from it. We have only to look at the United States to see that. Everywhere a combination of globalisation, economic and social change, mass migration, cultural disruption and financial crisis have posed formidable challenges to conventional politics, which seems impotent either to create the desirable or to prevent the undesirable. So membership of mainstream political parties has declined, election turnouts have fallen, and new political movements have emerged (Mair, 2013).

However, the EU has become a major aggravating factor for its member states. It has further removed power and legitimacy from elected national governments; and political, administrative and economic elites have, often eagerly, become part of an international caste decreasingly attuned to national electorates.

Major decisions take place at a further remove from democratic control, in the hands of the Commission, the Council of Ministers, or the European Central Bank. Generally they are taken in secret, often with little real discussion. As the historian of the EU John Gillingham has put it: 'Europe is governed today neither by its peoples nor by its ideals but by a bank board' (Gillingham, 2016, 239).

Moreover, while attempting to take independent powers away from its member states and their citizens, the EU itself has proved incapable of using those powers to solve the major problems of Europe, above all those that it has itself created through the structural flaws of the Eurozone.

Consequently, in all countries, unhappiness at the consequences of EU policies (including unemployment, mass migration and economic stagnation) has increased. In the absence of any genuine mechanism in the EU system for opposing and changing policies democratically, the result has been the growth of an angrier, more extreme brand of politics, whether of the extreme Left, the extreme Right, or some hybrid.

Furthermore, whether deliberately or inadvertently, the EU has encouraged regionalism by funding policies, by giving quasi-diplomatic recognition to regional authorities, and by creating a framework that encourages regions to believe they can act independently of their national government. Inevitably, this has in some cases mutated into separatism and has thus added another dimension to instability.

The effects across the European political scene are evident to all who look. Greece and Italy are mired in long-term economic stagnation, with the inevitable growth of political extremism. Spain is in continuing crisis over Catalonia. France has suddenly been reduced to turmoil by a spontaneous popular revolt against budgetary constraints required by the EU. Belgium and even France face separatist movements. The United Kingdom has seen the growth of Scottish nationalism. At the time of writing, minority governments or unstable coalitions are unsteadily in power in 14 EU states – half the total -- including Spain, Sweden, Denmark, Belgium, Lithuania, Estonia, the Czech Republic, Ireland, Portugal, the Netherlands – and of course the United Kingdom (*Le Monde,* 27 Dec. 2018).

Is there a remedy? It is hard to see one, especially with another bout of financial instability threatening the Eurozone. But there is a prudent course for the United Kingdom: to withdraw from a system which it cannot expect to influence, and to make serious efforts to strengthen its own economic, social and political fabric. Unlike many acts condemned as 'populist', the Brexit vote in 2016 was one of hope in the nation, its democracy and its institutions, and its first effect was to stabilise the British political scene, most obviously by eliminating Ukip, whose previous voters migrated back to the two main parties, Conservative and Labour.

Britain's political stability at stake

When Britain voted in the 2016 Referendum, the arguments for leaving were less pressing that they are now. This is partly because the prospects for the EU itself are now gloomier. Partly too (at least in the eyes of some) because the EU has revealed itself to be a more antagonistic and intractable partner than optimists (including, it would seem, Theresa May) expected: why, then, would we wish to remain part of a system that has seemed to treat us with such hostility? But most importantly of all is that our own political stability has been called into question by the continuing struggle over Brexit.

For the first time for more than a century, part of the political establishment, with the support of vocal elements in business, the media and the intelligentsia, have refused to accept the legitimacy of a legal referendum vote, confirmed in a general election.

Had Scotland voted for independence in its earlier referendum in 2014, it is unimaginable that there would have been a comparable attempt to overturn the result. The reasons for Remainer intransigence are manifold: personal interest, political opportunism, and bruised vanity certainly; though also genuine fear verging on panic at the supposed economic and political consequences. Underlying these feelings seems to be scepticism about the nation's ability to manage its own affairs.

Whatever the motives, they have been expressed in often inflammatory language, sometimes with undisguised contempt for supposedly less educated voters, and with the use of arguments and tactics that undermine the legitimacy of democratic politics as practised for generations. Even if the benefits of Brexit were quite small (and the disadvantages of EU membership similarly marginal), the question of the governance of the country that has arisen since 2016 makes the issue one of profound importance.

My 'journey'

For my part, I was hesitant about the vote in 2016; and I previously believed that a compromise that gave Britain some sort of associate membership of the EU would prove acceptable. But given the developments since the Referendum, I believe far more strongly that a clear and unambiguous Brexit has become necessary to resolve the issue with minimum political damage now and in the future. An ambiguous or duplicitous outcome would certainly perpetuate our present discontents. If a clear and legal popular vote were actually to be overridden or reversed, unknown dangers for our national cohesion and democratic legitimacy would be created.

Moreover, there would be serious implications for the rest of the EU. It is notorious that in other countries (including Denmark, Ireland, Holland and even France) where referenda produced an outcome unacceptable to the European political elite, it was either re-run or circumvented. Few people, I think, would have believed such an outcome possible in Britain, given its deeply rooted tradition of government by consent, and no less, its established scepticism about the European Union and its aims. But if despite everything Brexit were to be blocked, it would show that, whatever law and treaty might say, leaving the EU by mutual consent is not possible for any nation.

Historians, of whom I am one, rightly hesitate to predict the future. Given the present disquieting state of Europe, however, it seems safe to predict that a defeat of Brexit would not lead to the permanent triumph of a 'European super-state' or to the disappearance of Euroscepticism. Rather, it would mean that rejection of the EU no longer had a legal and peaceful outlet. That would be a dangerous prospect.

About the contributor

Robert Tombs is Emeritus Professor of French History at Cambridge, and a Fellow of St John's College. He is a specialist in French political history and Franco-British relations. His authored, co-authored or edited books include *Paris, bivouac des révolutions* (2014), *That Sweet Enemy: The French and the British from the Sun King to the Present* (2007), and *Britain and France in Two World Wars: Truth, Myth and Memory* (2013). His most recent book is *The English and Their History* (2014). He is co-editor of the website *Briefings for Brexit*.

Chapter 4

Why economists can and should disagree about everything...including Brexit

It is time for economists to stop pretending there is a consensus that Brexit can only have negative effects on the UK economy and to start focusing on how best to exploit the potential benefits of life outside the EU. Professor David Paton expands

Economists are famous for never being able to agree about anything. Indeed, it is the only discipline for which the Nobel Prize has been awarded to two people for saying exactly the opposite thing. In fact, it has happened twice: Myrdal and Von Hayek in 1974 and then, in 2013, Fama and Schiller.

Given this, the response of economists to Brexit has been somewhat curious. There is a perception that the profession is united in agreeing that leaving the EU will lead to significant losses under any scenario. One pre-election poll claimed that 88 per cent of economists thought that UK GDP would be negatively affected by Brexit[1]. Paul Johnson of the Institute for Fiscal Studies summed the situation up in this way: "With one or two very ideologically aligned exceptions, all economists take the view that from an economic point of view Brexit is going to be damaging."[2]

Many economists argued that a vote to leave would in itself trigger immediate damaging effects. For example, Treasury economists notoriously predicted there would be an immediate recession and unemployment would increase by half a million (HM Treasury, 2016). Of course, we now know that such Domesday forecasts were completely wide of the mark: since the 2016 referendum, unemployment has decreased to historic low levels whilst, far from the UK entering recession, GDP growth has been steady. Indeed, having lagged behind our key European competitors during 2017, the UK has now leapfrogged over Germany, France and Italy in the growth league tables.[3]

The failure of the short-term predictions does not seem to have caused much embarrassment amongst economists. Rather, many have doubled down, even implying that those economists who see potential benefits from Brexit are some sort of extremist fringe. 'Misleading nonsense' was the colourful description by the LSE's Dr Thomas Sampson about dissenting analysis suggesting the economy could actually gain from a clean break with the EU.[4]

The consensus myth

Perhaps, most shamefully, in 2016 the Royal Economic Society put in a formal complaint to the BBC about airtime being given to Economists for Free Trade, one of the most prominent groups of Brexit-supporting economists (RES, 2016). Unsurprisingly the BBC rejected the complaint, but the idea that the main representative organisation for economists should seek to censor views of its own members because they do not go along with the consensus is scarcely credible. In years to come, this will surely be seen as a stain on the reputation of an eminent organisation.

Even if it were true that economists are united in believing there are benefits from leaving the EU, it would hardly be something to boast about. Such a lack of diversity of opinion would mean the profession was in a very sorry state indeed. In fact, although economists with a more favourable view of Brexit may be in a minority, work such as Wyman and Petrescu (2017) and Coutts, Gudgin and Buchanan (2018) demonstrate convincingly that the idea of a consensus is a myth.

What's the argument?

At the heart of the economic arguments lies the effect of EU membership on trade and competitiveness. The EU Customs Union and Single Market are designed to make trade easier between EU countries, something standard economic theory suggests should benefit the economy. On the other hand, the Customs Union raises trade costs between EU and non-EU countries in a way which is likely to have a negative effect.

In most cases, EU tariffs are relatively low, but there are important exceptions in sectors such as food, cars, footwear and clothing. Tariffs (as well as quota restrictions) provide a high level of protection to EU producers, something which will tend to have deleterious long run effects on productivity.

A further issue is that the regulatory approach of the single market means that all companies have to comply with EU regulations whether not they export to the rest of the EU. As a result, any inefficiency in single market regulations is likely to raise costs of at least some UK firms.

The costs and benefits of leaving

It is clear that *a priori* there are likely to be costs and benefits from leaving the EU. A post-Brexit trading relationship which is very close to current arrangements may limit the costs of leaving but is also likely to limit our ability to reap the benefits. It might be perfectly reasonable to come to a judgement that costs will exceed the benefits in any or indeed all scenarios. But we need to remember that the effects outlined above are difficult to measure meaning that a forecast of even just one factor will have a very broad confidence interval. When predictions of several different effects are combined to arrive at an overall forecast, the level of uncertainty is very high indeed.

The approach of much economic forecasting has involved modelling the costs of Brexit in some detail whilst treating potential benefits in a cursory fashion. A prime example is the recent Treasury modelling which predicts that leaving without a trade deal with the EU will result in GDP per capita being about 8 per cent lower in 2035 that would be expected if the UK stayed in the EU (HM Treasury, 2018).

The order of magnitude of the predicted effect seems implausible on the face of it given that total EU trade accounts for only 12 per cent of total UK GDP (Minford, 2018). But the result is a direct effect of the assumptions underlying the Treasury model. For example, they work on the basis that UK firms trading with the EU will face additional non-tariff barriers such as border control costs of up to 15 per cent of the value of trade, despite the fact that the vast majority of customs checks are carried out very economically via electronic procedures. On the other hand, the Treasury simply assumes that the benefit from firms being regulated by the UK rather than having to follow single market rules is essentially zero.

Unsurprisingly, such an approach leads to predictions of big losses under Brexit. It is not that this is a completely implausible outcome, but economic forecasting is notoriously unreliable and economists need to be honest about the assumptions on which their models are predicated.

They should debate the merits of alternative modelling approaches and assumptions without pretending that one side of the argument has a monopoly of truth about an inherently unpredictable process. For example, alternative modelling by Minford (2018), using a similar framework to that used by the Treasury but with different assumptions, concludes that leaving the EU without a deal is likely to lead to a significant boost to long term economic growth.

One key assumption in many of the negative forecasts is that inward foreign direct investment (FDI) to the UK will be significantly hit by Brexit. A commonly cited source for this is the work of Bruno, Campos, Estrin and Tian (2016) who estimate the average effect of EU membership on FDI to be 22 per cent. They then go on to infer that leaving the EU will cause UK FDI to drop by at least 22 per cent. If true, clearly it would have severe consequences for long-term economic growth.

However, their estimates are derived from panel data econometric analysis driven by the effects of EU membership of countries joining the EU between 1985 and 2013, the majority being Eastern European transition economies.

Relative to the UK, these countries have smaller economies, traditionally low rates of FDI and had recently undergone a significant transformation from state-controlled to market economies. This is hardly a good basis for estimating the impact of the UK leaving the EU on FDI. For example, it is reasonable to think that the effect on FDI of former Eastern bloc countries joining the EU would be particularly big given the requirements for EU membership in terms of institutional development and economic stability. Add into the mix other UK-specific factors such as the language, a stable political system, a legal system, and global influence which make it a particularly attractive proposition for overseas investors and there are very good reasons to believe that the impact of EU membership on FDI for countries joining between 1985 and 2013 will be an order of magnitude higher than the impact of the UK leaving the EU.

Can Brexit be good for FDI?

In fact, there could also be positive effects on FDI from Brexit, for example if multinationals think it important to make sure they have a foothold in the strategically important UK market when our ties with the EU are loosened.

The early empirical evidence on this point is mixed. Serwicka and Tamberi (2018) conclude that the referendum did indeed have a negative impact on FDI in 2017. On the other hand, the most recent data from the OECD finds that actual FDI into the UK in the first half of 2018 has been at record levels, higher than every country in the world apart from China.[5] Looking to the future, the Kearney FDI surveys suggest international confidence in long term UK FDI prospects is actually higher than before the referendum.[6]

We are unlikely to understand the full impact of the Referendum and Brexit itself on FDI for some time to come. But it is misleading for forecasters simply to assume that FDI will be significantly hit without at least being honest about the range of possible outcomes.

In conclusion

A unique policy change like Brexit has few precedents from which we can draw lessons which makes forecasting particularly hard and uncertain. Under the new policy environment, entrepreneurial firms are likely to identify and exploit opportunities which are not on the radar at the moment. Economists need to be frank about the challenges this brings and present their forecasts with humility and caution. It will no longer do just to assert that the profession is united and that any upside to Brexit can be ignored.

Leaving the EU will bring both risks and opportunities. Rather than trying to refight the referendum battles, it is time for economists to engage with the potential benefits of Brexit in a more balanced and constructive way.

Notes

1. Ipsos Mori poll, 28th May 2016, www.ipsos.com/ipsos-mori/en-uk/economists-views-brexit
2. Business Insider, 26th Jan 2018, www.businessinsider.com/ifs-director-paul-johnson-brexit-is-going-to-be-damaging-2018-1?r=UK&IR=T
3. www.oecd.org/economy/gdp-growth-third-quarter-2018-oecd.htm
4. City A.M. Debate: Is the Economists for Free Trade £135bn figure realistic?, 16th Dec, 2017 www.cityam.com
5. www.gov.uk/government/news/uk-leading-europe-for-fdi-as-fox-hunts-future-investors-in-china
6. www.atkearney.com/foreign-direct-investment-confidence-index/full-report

References

Bruno, Randolph, Nauro Campos, Saul Estrin and Meng Tian (2016) 'Gravitating towards Europe: an econometric analysis of the FDI effects of EU membership', *Technical Appendix to 'The Impact of Brexit on Foreign Investment in the UK'* http://cep.lse.ac.uk/pubs/download/brexit03_technical_paper.pdf

Coutts, Ken, Graham Gudgin and Jordan Buchanan (2018), 'How the economics profession got it wrong on Brexit', *Working Paper* 493 (Jan), Centre for Business Research.

HM Treasury (2018), *EU Exit: long-term analysis*, Cm 9742 (Nov).

HM Treasury (2016), *The immediate economic impact of leaving the EU*, Cm 9292 (May).

Minford, Patrick (2018), 'Overview of Treasury Brexit Forecasts Published on 28 November 2018', *Submission to the Treasury Committee* (Dec).

Royal Economic Society (2016), 'Academic economists and the media – the RES complains to the BBC', Newsletter (Oct).

Serwicka, Ilona and Nicolo Tamberi (2018), 'Not Backing Britain: FDI Inflows since the Brexit Referendum', *Briefing Paper* 23, Oct, http://blogs.sussex.ac.uk/uktpo/publications/not-backing-britain-fdi-inflows-since-the-brexit-referendum/

Wyman, Philip B and Alina I Petrescu (2017) *Was there really an Economic Consensus on Brexit?* in, *The Economics of Brexit*, Palgrave Macmillan, pp1-50.

About the contributor

Professor David Paton holds the Chair of Industrial Economics at Nottingham University Business School. He is co-editor of the International Journal of the Economics of Business and is a member of Economists for Free Trade. His research on topics such as the economics of cricket, gambling taxation, productivity, teenage pregnancy and the post-Brexit economy has been published in a wide range of outlets. David has provided advice to a range of government departments including DCMS, HM Customs and Excise, DTI and the National Audit Office.

Chapter 5

How the economics profession got it wrong on Brexit

The economics profession, which failed to predict the banking crisis, has also failed in forecasting the economic impact of Brexit. The short-term forecasts published during the referendum campaign, were clearly overly-pessimistic and a replication of long-term forecasts reveal important flaws which exaggerate pessimism, argue Ken Coutts and Graham Gudgin

A wide range of reports estimating the impact of Brexit were published by official bodies and academic and consultancy groups during the Brexit referendum campaign of 2016. The Ashcroft poll[1] undertaken immediately after the referendum indicated that among those who voted to remain the likely negative economic impact of Brexit was a major factor in their vote. It thus seems likely that these economic impact reports influenced the referendum vote. They are also likely to remain influential in informing views on the potential long-term consequences of a range of Brexit trade arrangements.

Despite a lack of evidence that membership of the EU has improved living standards in the EU (Coutts et al, 2018), these reports all asserted that leaving the EU would damage the UK economy both in the run-up to departure and in the longer term. The most influential of these reports are from HM Treasury, the Bank of England and the OECD, all of which published predictions for both the short and long terms, and the LSE's Centre for Economic Performance which estimated long-term impacts alone.

The short-term impact of Brexit

The Treasury's short-term predictions for Brexit are now notorious because key aspects have proved hopelessly wide of the mark (HM Treasury 2016b). The Treasury modelled a link between the economic confidence of businesses and households and their subsequent spending behaviour including business investment. The assumption made about the likely hit to confidence was incorrect and the associated predicted negative impacts were thus greatly exaggerated.

The Treasury's short-term prediction, even in its milder scenario using what it calls 'cautious' assumptions, was *'four quarters of negative growth'*. After two years (i.e. by 2018) *'GDP would be around 3.6 per cent lower'*. *'The fall in the value of the pound would be around 12 per cent'*, and *'unemployment would increase by around 500,000'*. The Bank of England and IMF agreed that recession was possible.

A letter[2] signed by more than 175 economists including 12 (mainly American) Nobel Laureates, three peers, five knights, three CBEs, one OBE, two Pro-Vice-Chancellors, 81 professors and eight assistant professors, made less precise but essentially similar claims.

Other than the fall in the pound (which could have been influenced by the predictions themselves) these forecasts were dramatically wrong. There has been no recession and unemployment has not risen. Indeed, unemployment has fallen by a quarter of a million since the referendum.

An error of three-quarters of a million in a two-year forecast for unemployment must count as one of the most egregious in the history of economic forecasting. Excuses that remedial action by the Bank of England saved the day are not credible. Nor is it plausible that the delay in the UK calling of the EU's article 50 moderated the outcome. The pro-Brexit Economists for Free Trade group also made short-term forecasts and overestimated post-referendum growth in GDP in 2016 and 2017 by 1.2 per cent. This compares with a Treasury underestimate of 2.9-4.9 per cent and an average under-estimate across all forecasting groups of 2.1 per cent (EFT, 2018).

The long-term impact of Brexit

The core of the long-term analyses was an attempt to estimate how much extra trade the UK does within the EU as a result of its membership of the

EU. In each case an assumption was made that much or all of this extra trade would eventually be lost when the UK leaves the EU. These estimates were made using either gravity models or a computable general equilibrium models, both widely used in economic analysis.

Gravity models use the size of economies and their distance apart (and a few other relevant factors) to predict how much trade will occur between any two countries. This provides a baseline to estimate how much extra trade occurs between EU members due to their membership of the EU.

The key flaw in the Treasury analysis (HM Treasury, 2016a) was to calculate an *average* trade impact across all 28 EU members. The UK, which is the only large EU member to export more outside the EU than within, has much lower gains in trade from EU membership[3]. The UK thus has much less to lose even if it is assumed that all existing trade gains from membership will be lost after leaving.

We know from an internal 2005 Treasury paper obtained through a freedom of information request that the Treasury understood this flaw, but it made no mention of this understanding in its 2016 report. The extra UK trade with the EU (and hence trade liable to be lost due to Brexit) predicted in the Treasury's 2016 paper was 115 per cent. In the 2005 paper it was only 7 per cent for the UK alone. Much of even that small trade gain from EU membership was offset by diversion of trade from outside the EU.

The Treasury speculated in its 2005 paper that UK trade gained less from EU membership than did other EU states because of the UK's greater history of trade openness. This is an important point, not mentioned in the Treasury's 2016 report. In contrast with the UK, with its main focus outside the EU, some EU members, particularly the newer members, do more than 80 per cent of their trade within the EU.

An important additional aspect of the Treasury and other analyses is a link between trade and productivity. This accounts for around half of the negative impact on GDP calculated by the Treasury in its 2016 report. In common with the Nobel-prize winning US economist Paul Krugman[4] we doubt that that such a link exists among advanced economies.

The evidence cited by the Treasury uses old data and depends heavily on the experience of emerging economies. Our update of the data for the link between goods trade and productivity, focussing only on the richer OECD economies, indicates no relationship whatsoever (Coutts et al., 2005, p22).

The Treasury has subsequently dropped its gravity model approach and adopted a different model. It initially declined to identify the new model, which we now know is based on a CGE model from Purdue University in the USA (HM Government, 2018). Computable General Equilibrium (CGE) models use economic theory to directly model the behaviour of 'representative' companies and households but in order to do so in a mathematically tractable way make a series of unrealistic assumptions. These models are common in the international trade literature despite their highly unrealistic assumptions. Their use in a trade context depends heavily on what is assumed about the extra costs due to tariff and non-tariff barriers and the 'elasticities' used to convert these costs into losses of trade.

The estimated impacts of a no-deal Brexit in the Treasury's November 2018 report remain large, negative, and much the same as in their 2016 report (HM Government, 2018). Our own initial review of this new Treasury report suggests that once again the estimates of the impact of Brexit are exaggerated in a negative direction.

Estimates of the size of non-tariff barriers are inappropriately large for the UK economy in which all firms are already fully compliant with EU regulations and in which customs costs can be minimised with modern customs arrangements. The elasticities linking extra trade costs and loss of trade volumes are built into the Purdue model and appear to be very large, and many times larger than those observed in the UK over recent years for the impact of exchange rate changes on trade volumes.

The Purdue elasticities suggest that even small increases in costs will result in large losses of trade with the EU. These important assumptions are not discussed in the new Treasury report despite its 70-page technical annex (H M Government, 2018). An academic estimate (Ciuriac et al, 2017) using the same Purdue model calculated negative impacts which were only one third as large as the Treasury's.

This new approach adopted by the Treasury is similar to that used in 2016 by the LSE's Centre For Economic Performance (CEP) (Dhingra et al, 2017) to estimate the long-term impact of Brexit.

The CEP does not predict Brexit impacts through time but instead provides a single estimate of settled long-term impact. The calculated long-term impacts for 'no deal' due to tariff and non-tariff barriers between the UK and EU, are tiny, amounting to only 1.3 per cent of GDP. These are however increased by adding an impact for future divergence in regulations. Future divergences are not however an impact of Brexit per se but depend on hypothetical future policy decisions of UK governments. A further large addition is made for the productivity link which as stated above we do not believe exists.

Another main class of economic model. 'structural econometric models' does not attempt to model the behaviour of the 'representative' firm or household but instead uses actual data over time to estimate aggregate relationships between such things as household incomes and consumer expenditure.

Estimates of the economic impact of Brexit using these models tend to generate smaller negative impacts. An example is the study undertaken by Cambridge Econometrics (CE) for the Mayor of London (Cambridge Econometrics, 2018). The results showed a small negative impact for per capita GDP in the UK and a positive impact for London. CE appears to have lacked the courage of its own convictions and did not emphasise these points in its conclusions. As a result, its optimism was not reported in the media.

Other approaches examine the potential direct impact of Brexit on trade but do not use macro-economic models to go further in order to assess the impact of trade losses on aggregate GDP.

Once again, the approach requires estimates of the extra costs of tariff and non-tariff barriers, usually at a detailed sectoral level, plus sectoral elasticities to convert the extra costs into impacts on trade volumes.

Once more, much depends on how the non-tariff barriers are calculated and what elasticities are used. Different data on non-tariff barriers and for elasticities can result in widely different estimates even from the same authors (Lawless and Morganroth 2016, Lawless and Studnicka, 2017, Kee and Nicita, 2017).

Finally, a new Bank of England report was published in November 2018 (Bank of England, 2018). Its predictions were described as scenarios, but as Paul Krugman says, it was naïve at best not to know that these would be reported as forecasts of what would happen when the UK leaves the EU.

This Bank report uses a gravity model approach and appears to incorporate all of the flaws described above for the Treasury's 2016 long-term report. A former Bank of England Monetary Committee member called the report bogus[5] and Paul Krugman expressed great scepticism[6]. Both are strong Remainers.

Conclusions

This chapter has argued that flaws in the application of models, or in the reporting of the results, have exaggerated the negative impact of Brexit. This is particularly the case for the various reports by HM Treasury and we regard the Treasury's involvement in the Brexit debate as little short of a constitutional outrage.

It is obvious that Treasury civil servants, serving political masters with strong political positions on Brexit, cannot be independent or unbiased. A former Cabinet secretary has said that in his time the Treasury would never have been allowed to contribute in this way.

The Treasury's role, and that of other official bodies, has been protected by the technicality of the analysis. Few people outside the ranks of economic theorists and modellers are in a position to understand how the estimates of the economic impact of Brexit are generated.

Many politicians and others rely instead on the prestige of these organisations in a way that Michael Gove warned against during the referendum campaign[7].

The obvious failure of the short-term forecasts made in 2016 have weakened the already faltering public confidence in official forecasts, but the strongly partisan nature of the Brexit debate means that official predictions are still called in aid of the case against Brexit despite the poor record on the short-term forecasts.

The wider role of the economics profession is also important here. The Treasury, OECD, IMF and Bank of England and others have all used standard economic techniques.

The problem has usually been the way the techniques are used and the assumptions underlying their use in the context of Brexit. The techniques are however vulnerable to misuse, and the fact that the great majority of economists take one ideological side in the Brexit debate creates a situation in which criticism is absent or suppressed. In this context we need to explain that our own work replicating the Treasury analysis was undertaken by a four-person research group, of whom three voted Remain.

Notes

1. https://lordashcroftpolls.com/2016/06/how-the-united-kingdom-voted-and-why/
2. https://economistsforremain.org/
3. The only other exception is Malta which is geographically closer to North Africa than to Europe
4. https://www.nytimes.com/2018/11/30/opinion/brexit-borders-and-the-bank-of-england-wonkish.html
5. https://www.ftadviser.com/investments/2018/11/29/bank-forecasts-dismissed-as-bogus-by-former-rate-setter/
6. https://www.nytimes.com/2018/11/30/opinion/brexit-borders-and-the-bank-of-england-wonkish.html
7. https://www.huffingtonpost.co.uk/entry/michael-gove-accused-of-donald-trump-politics-in-feisty-sky-news-eu-referendum-tv-debate_uk_5751e4bde4b04a0827f1a12d?guccounter=1&guce_referrer_us=aHR0cHM6Ly93d3cuZ29vZ2xlLmNvbS88&guce_referrer_cs=QFQNRF9ladv219i2iw1Ghg 'I think the people of this country have had enough of experts from organisations with acronyms saying that they know what is best and consistently getting it wrong'.

References

Bank of England, (2018) EU Withdrawal Scenarios and Monetary and Financial Stability. Nov 28. Bank of England. https://www.bankofengland.co.uk/report/2018/eu-withdrawal-scenarios-and-monetary-and-financial-stability/

Cambridge Econometrics, (2018), Preparing for Brexit, Report for *Greater London Authority*, January. https://www.camecon.com/news/economic-impact-brexit-starkly-revealed-new-report/

Coutts K, Gudgin G and Buchanan J (2018) How the Economics Profession Got it Wrong on Brexit. University of Cambridge, Centre For Business Research, Working paper No. 493. http://www.cbr.cam.ac.uk/fileadmin/user_upload/centre-for-business-research/downloads/working-papers/wp493.pdf

Ciuriak, D and Dadkhah, A and Xiao, J, Brexit Trade Impacts: Alternative Scenarios (2017). https://ssrn.com/abstract=2981314 or http://dx.doi.org/10.2139/ssrn.2981314/

Dhingra, S., Huang, H., Ottaviano,G., Pessoa, J. P., Sampson, T., and van Reenan, J., (2017), The Costs and Benefits of Leaving the EU: the Trade Effects. CEP Discussion Paper No 1478 April. http://cep.lse.ac.uk/pubs/download/dp1478.pdf

HM Government (2018) EU Exit. Long-term Economic Analysis. November 2018. Cmnd 9742. https://assets.publishing.service.gov.uk/government/uploads/system/uploads/attachment_data/file/760484/28_November_EU_Exit_-_Long-term_economic_analysis__1_.pdf

HM Treasury, (2005), EU Membership and Trade. Internal Paper Unclassified. (Authors unknown) https://www.gov.uk/government/uploads/system/uploads/attachment_data/file/220968/foi_eumembership_trade.pdf/

HM Treasury, (2016a), H M Treasury Analysis: the long-term economic impact of UK membership and the alternatives, CM 9250, April. https://www.gov.uk/government/uploads/system/uploads/attachment_data/file/517415/treasury_analysis_economic_impact_of_eu_membership_web.pdf/H. M. Treasury, (2016b), The immediate economic impact of leaving the EU. Cmnd 9292. May. https://www.gov.uk/government/uploads/system/uploads/attachment_data/file/524967/hm_treasury_analysis_the_immediate_economic_impact_of_leaving_the_eu_web.pdf/

Lawless, M. and Morgenroth, E, (2016), The Product and Sector level Impact of a Hard Brexit across the EU, ESRI, working Paper no. 550, November.

Lawless, M. and Studnicka, Z., (2017), Potential Impact of WTO Tariffs on Cross-border Trade, InterTradeIreland, June.

http://www.intertradeireland.com/media/InterTradeIrelandPotenti
alImpactofWTOTariffsResearchReportFINAL.PDF/

Kee, H. L. and Nicita, A., (2017), Short Term Impact of Brexit on the UK's Exports of Goods. Vox Blog, World Bank and UNCTAD. https://voxeu.org/article/short-term-impact-brexit-uk-exports/

About the contributors

Graham Gudgin is Honorary Research Associate at the Centre For Business Research (CBR) in the Judge Business School at the University of Cambridge and Chief Economic Advisor at Policy Exchange in London. He was formerly Director of the Northern Ireland Economic Research Centre in Belfast and from 1998-2002 was Special Advisor to First Minister David Trimble in Northern Ireland and previously economics fellow at Selwyn College, Cambridge.

Ken Coutts is Honorary Research Associate at the Centre For Business Research (CBR) in the Judge Business School, Emeritus Assistant Director of Studies in the Faculty of Economics, and Life Fellow in Economics, Selwyn College, at the University of Cambridge. A member of the Cambridge Economic Policy Group in his younger career, led by the late Wynne Godley, his main interests are in macroeconomics, monetary and fiscal policy, trade, capital flows and balance of payments. He has published widely in these areas. He has also written extensively on the pricing behaviour of manufacturing industries in the UK and Australia. He is currently working with Graham Gudgin on a macro-economic model and forecasts for the UK economy and on the economic impact of Brexit.

Chapter 6

The default option of a World Trade Deal is the best available

Theresa May's proposed deal with the EU has hit massive opposition in Parliament, with no willingness from the EU side to revise it. It is time to recognise that we are headed towards the default option of no deal, or more accurately, an exit under WTO rules, better called a 'World Trade Deal'. What would this involve? Patrick Minford explains

First, we should dispose of the idea that Brexit means 'crashing out' in a 'disorderly' way. Both we and the EU are now preparing for this option, as we must, since it is now highly likely.

The implication is that neither we nor they wish to see any disorder, for example with rights being undefined for each other's citizens or for a lack of over-flying and landing agreements for aircraft. As it happens, painstaking agreement has already been reached on these matters either in the existing withdrawal agreement or separately, so these agreements simply need to be translated into or taken forward as, separate bilateral agreements in conjunction with a no (trade) deal.

Second, we need to be clear that leaving under WTO rules implies no disorder in trade relations, since these are precisely what WTO rules regulate to create order.

The key rules

There are two key rules that apply here.

The first compels both sides to run a 'seamless' border with respect to each other: that means no unnecessary delays and the standard customs service with pre-clearance via computerised submission of cargo details In practice these rules mean border costs are trivial (Ambuhl, 2018, computes them at 0.1 per cent of trade value at the Swiss border).

The second prevents either side from discriminating against the other on export goods standards. This means that if their exports satisfy our standards, we cannot suddenly pretend they do not for some trumped-up reason. Nor they with our exports. Of course, currently we both have identical standards. If in future our standards start to diverge, we can be sure that exporters on both sides will continue to comply. as all exporters do in all their export markets.

So, there will be no disorder at the border because it is illegal under WTO rules.

'Big gains from a clean Brexit'

But there will be big gains to the UK economy from leaving the EU cleanly under the World Trade Deal. Furthermore, after we have left, we can agree to forge a free-trade agreement with the EU under WTO Article24, under which we would keep our existing zero tariffs against each other until the deal was done.

What then are the whole range of economic benefits we estimate from achieving a clean Brexit – i.e. leaving the Single Market and the Customs Union, regaining control over our borders, laws, and regulations, freeing ourselves from the European Court of Justice, and having the freedom to establish our own trading relationships with the rest of the world? Over the past two years, I have reported at length on the long run effects of such a 'Clean Brexit' (Minford, 2017). I briefly recapitulate the arguments and findings from my research with my co-authors at Cardiff University.

A 'Clean Brexit' produces long-run gains from four main sources:

1. Moving to free trade with non-EU countries that currently face high EU protection in goods trade;
2. Substituting UK-based regulation for EU-based single market regulation;

3. Ending the large subsidy the 'four freedoms' forces the UK to give to EU unskilled immigrants;
4. Ending our budget contribution to the EU.

The gains under (1) come about because elimination of the EU's protection lowers consumer prices and increases competition in our home market, so raising productivity across our industries. With the economy at full employment and a flexible exchange rate, any jobs lost in industries where higher productivity releases labour will be offset by extra jobs in other (unprotected) industries where productivity is already high and where demand is projected to expand.

For our calculations on our Cardiff World Trade Model (Minford et al, 2015, chapter 4; Minford and Xu, 2018), we assume that protection leading to higher prices of 10 per cent in both food and manufactures is eliminated (the detailed research noted above shows prices inside the EU in both sectors currently are some 20 per cent higher than world market prices). Our estimates are that consumer prices will fall by 8 per cent and GDP will rise by 4 per cent.

For (2), we rely on models of the economy developed by Cardiff researchers (see Minford et al, 2015, chapter 2) that assess the effects of regulation on the economy via their effect in raising business costs. We estimate that EU regulation has reduced GDP by around 6 per cent; and that probably about a third of this can be reversed giving us a projected gain of 2 per cent of GDP, or a growth rate 0.15 per cent per annum faster over the next 15 years.

For (3), we have examined the costs to the taxpayer of EU unskilled immigrants owing to their entitlement to the full range of tax credits and other benefits, including free education and healthcare (Ashton, MacKinnon and Minford, 2016). A further effect is that wages of UK unskilled workers are depressed; this represents a transfer from unskilled workers to the consumers who use their products.

A further relevant distributional element is that the taxpayer burden and wage effect are both highly localised in areas of immigration. From these costs, we find that Brexit would save 0.2 per cent of GDP in taxpayer costs. Furthermore, there would be a particular benefit to UK low-income households of about 15 per cent of their living costs from the combination of ending this unskilled immigrant subsidy and the trade-led reduction in the CPI (MacKinnon, 2018). For (4), we have followed the standard calculations made by the Office of Budget Responsibility and others, arriving at around 0.6 per cent of GDP.

In total these four elements create a rise in GDP in the long term over the next decade and a half of about 7 per cent, which is equivalent to an average rise in the growth rate of around 0.5% per annum.

The Treasury – 'the heart of Remain'

But, you may rightly say, the Treasury is totally against a World Trade Deal, so why is that? Boris Johnson, when Foreign Secretary, discovered this and has since called the Treasury 'the heart of Remain'.

After discarding use of its widely criticised 'gravity-like' model used in the initial 'Project Fear' Referendum forecasts, the Treasury has now adopted use of a Computable General Equilibrium (CGE) model (GTAP from Purdue University) that is similar in approach to the World Trade Model at Cardiff University that we use – but it has inputted into this blameless model some ludicrous assumptions (let us ignore here their migration assumptions under which the flow of migrants is abruptly cut off, when it is generally agreed that skilled migrants will be flexibly treated and unskilled migrants will be allowed in temporarily and without access to state benefits).

Based on the latest Treasury Report and its Technical Annex , the assumptions are flawed in two fundamental ways:

a) They assume there will suddenly spring up at the EU-UK border large border costs and trade barriers which kill off our EU trade in a costly way. But as we have already seen, this is illegal nonsense, pure and simple.

b) They assume we will fail to do much in the way of free trade agreements with the non-EU world. But in this they contradict the government's very own policies. So this makes no sense either. For more details see Economists for Free Trade (2018).

Why the Treasury and other civil servants have chosen to believe this nonsense no-one can say. It might be because the CBI and large manufacturing companies like Nissan, that dislike the extra competition Brexit will bring, have lobbied hard and brutally against Brexit. It may be out of pure prejudice or fear of any changes in the status quo. Who can tell?

One thing is clear however. Leaving the EU cleanly allows us to move our policies to free trade, and good regulation, regaining our economic sovereignty. In all our history these policies have served us well. and they will do so again today. This is why in the Referendum, there was a majority for Brexit. The latest spurious Project Fear arguments from the establishment will not succeed in putting us off now any more than they did in the referendum itself.

References

Ambühl, M. (2018) 'Where Next on Brexit? Lessons from the Swiss Model', Policy Exchange presentation, London, 19 April.

Ashton, P, MacKinnon, N. and Minford, P. (2016) 'The economics of unskilled immigration',http://www.economistsforfreetrade.com/the-economics-of-unskilled-immigration

Civil Service (2018a) 'EU Exit analysis- a cross-Whitehall briefing', Powerpoint slides, pp.27. https://www.parliament.uk/documents /commons-committees/Exiting-the-European-Union/17-19/Cross-Whitehall-briefing/EU-Exit-Analysis-Cross-Whitehall-Briefing.pdf

Trade-Deal-exit-from-the-EU-may-be-best-for-the-UK-Final-15.06.18.pdf

Economists for Free Trade (2018)'An overview of the Treasury's new Brexit forecasts', https://www.economistsforfreetrade.com/publication/an-overview-of-the-treasurys-new-brexit-forecasts/

HM Treasury (2016) 'HM Treasury analysis: the long-term economic impact of EU membership and the alternatives', Ref: ISBN 978-1-4741-3089-9, PU1908, Cm 9250PDF, 8.97

MacKinnon, N. (2018) 'Immigration: a central Brexit issue', https://www.economistsforfreetrade.com/wp-content/uploads/2018/11/Immigration-a-central- Brexit-issue.pdf

Minford, P., with Gupta, Le V., Mahambare, V. and Xu, Y. (2015) Should Britain leave the EU? An economic analysis of a troubled relationship, second edition, December 2015, pp. 197, (Cheltenham, 2015)

Minford, P. and Xu, Y. (2018) 'Classical or gravity: which trade model best matches the UK facts?' Open Economies Review, July 2018, Volume 29(3), pp 579–611 https://link.springer.com/content/pdf/10.1007%2Fs11079-017-9470-z.pdf

About the contributor

Patrick Minford is a macro-economist who holds the chair of Applied Economics at Cardiff University where he directs the Julian Hodge Institute of Applied Macroeconomics. Before academic life he was an economic adviser to Her Majesty's Treasury's External Division and editor of the National Institute Review. From 1976 to 1997, he was the Edward Gonner Professor of Applied Economics at Liverpool University where he founded and directed the Liverpool Research Group in Macroeconomics; this built the 'Liverpool Model' of the UK, which was influential in forecasting and policy analysis during the 1980s.

He was a member of Monopolies and Mergers Commission 1990-96; and one of the HM Treasury's Panel of Forecasters ('6 Wise Men') January 1993-December 1996. He was made a CBE for services to economics in 1996. His economic interests include monetary, trade, labour market and macro economics and modelling. Recent publications include: *Should Britain leave the EU? An economic analysis of a troubled relationship*, (with S. Gupta, V. Mahambare, V. Le and Y. Xu)

Chapter 7

The case for Brexit in December 2018

There is an unexpected new argument for Brexit since the 2016 referendum Leave victory, to be added to the two long-standing ones, says Gwythian Prins

Until June 2016 and for the preceding four decades, the case for Brexit was straightforwardly a game of two halves. But since then it has divided unexpectedly – and venomously – into three parts.

The long-standing two-part case was that, on the one hand, Brexit corrects geo-political and cultural errors that have constrained British power and influence in the world and that have disfigured British politics, breeding resentment and mistrust, for a generation. On the other, since committing the greatest geo-political error in modern European history by trying to force political union through the agency of a premature single currency, the 'project of European union' has been steadily advancing into the zone of risk of its own collapse.

So conscious uncoupling from this rapidly imploding elite project was an eminently wise decision by voters who are more clear-sighted and less emotionally and, in many cases, financially committed to the EU, than the echo-chamber of experts. Who wishes to be shackled to a structural failure?

Argument one: Brexit restores normal service – geopolitically and culturally

President De Gaulle was, of course, correct in seeking to keep Great Britain out.!! Rightly, he anticipated that if allowed into the hen-house, the British fox would wreak havoc. And so it did. Throughout our membership, the British aim was consistently to seek the maximum benefits for Britain with the minimum constraints on sovereign action. In this aim, Britain and France were, and are, indistinguishable. What has always differed, however, is the ruthless single-mindedness with which any French politician or official has pursued French national interests, compared to the limp performance of their British counterparts, especially – bizarrely – since the decision to leave in 2016; and, of course, long-term British and French national interests are systemically divergent where not in actual conflict.

Mrs Thatcher put her finger on it. What was the driving force of the project for European federation? That the French feared the Germans – and so did the Germans. The Cambridge international public lawyer Philip Allott once put the conundrum of differing motivation with eminent clarity: the German ambition was for *order* – for the multiple bonds of Lilliput to tie down German destructive tendencies in a welcome surrender of sovereignty. The French ambition was for *security* after the humiliations of serial defeats and occupation by Germany since 1870; and the British ambition, unchanging since victory in the first truly global war against the French at the turn of the 18th and 19th centuries, was and is for *freedom.*

These three strands could, for a time, be entwined. But they were coiled in permanent tension and in the end, were bound to fly apart. That moment of unbinding occurred with the introduction of the Euro in 1999 and became irreparable when, in 2005, the rejection of the EU 'Constitution' by a huge margin by the Netherlands, the oldest continental bastion of freedom, was circumvented.[i]

Just as de Gaulle feared, the arrival of the British in Brussels disrupted *le jardin des français.* During the period of British membership, in three ways we successfully obstructed the progress towards federal union which is the guiding motive in every Brussels action.

First of all, British diplomacy succeeded for a period in diluting the control of the Franco-German core by promoting enlargement, especially to the East after the end of the Cold War in 1989.

Secondly, as Europe's pre-eminent military and especially intelligence power, long-standing ambitions to create a Military EU to contest Nato and the Anglosphere, were frustrated for 50 years, from the failed Pleven Plan of 1950 until 2016. (Military EU took off with a vengeance in November 2016 and on Armistice Day 2018, at Verdun, President Macron openly identified the USA as one of the EU's potential enemies. That Military EU now poses a mortal threat to British national security is central to the third argument, below.)

Thirdly, by virtue of our command and control of the world language, the British anglicised the Brussels administration: a gift that, to the vexation of French speakers, will endure long after our political departure.

But all this was a pyrrhic victory because, as the Attorney General Geoffrey Cox resonantly reminded the 2018 Conservative Party Conference, the price of these positional successes, much vaunted and still mourned by unreconciled Remainers, was always too high.

Joining the EEC cost Britain the peerless advantages of Commonwealth preference and cost the Commonwealth 40 years delay in development of the Anglosphere's fullest potentials. It is the Queen's signal service to her nation that during the decades of deviation from the British norm, she has skilfully preserved the goodwill of the Commonwealth and, thereby, the opportunity for the prodigal to return.

Within the global Anglosphere, the deep trust within our central security alliance – the 'Five Eyes' Intelligence alliance of Australia, Canada, New Zealand, the UK and USA – stands living witness to where our prime cultural affinities really lie.

The experience of reluctant membership within an inherently resentful organism simply demonstrated the enduring truth of Winston Churchill's 1930 observation that Britain was with, but not of, continental Europe: 'linked but not compromised' (cit Leach (2004: 25). Therefore, one of the most positive consequences for all parties of Britain ceasing to be under any power of the EU is that it will permit resumption of the geo-political norm in our relationships of over three centuries, never more lucidly expressed than by Viscount Castlereagh in his Great State Paper of 5 May 1820 (reproduced Ward & Gooch, 1923: 622-33).

This is that only a truly independent Britain can (and will) come to the rescue of the continental nations from their latest experiment with imperial or autocratic federalism, whether by Napoleon, the Kaiser, Hitler or now, the rapidly imploding autocracy of the EC's nomenklatura, led by Martin Selmayr, the EU's real boss.

The other price that was too high was that any positional advantages were far outweighed by compromise of the British Constitution through loss of sovereignty. Administrative law is reeled into the one way ratchet of the EU *acquis communautaire* and the Common Law becomes submerged by the rising tide of the powers of an institutionally federalising European Court of Justice, whose effect upon British justice and courts the great judge Lord Denning once famously described (in Bulmer v. Bollinger [1974] Ch. 401): "It flows into the estuaries and up the rivers. It cannot be held back."

Even Britain's narrow escape from joining the euro single currency, whose slow poison is increasingly the most likely agent likely to precipitate the EU's early demise, does not offset the structural costs in progressive surrender of legal, political, administrative and economic sovereignty during the decades of membership, the unqualified recovery of which was the most prominent single shared motivation among those who voted to leave in 2016. So why did we ever join?

The original decision was the consequence of a collective crisis of self confidence in the British Establishment, crystallised by the humiliation of the Suez debacle in 1956. The irresistible application of American power which ended the Franco-British operation at the very moment that Generals Massu and Stockwell has achieved their military objectives, fused with a long-standing declinist mood whose antecedents lay in appeasement in the 1930s.

Together they were instrumental in formalising a view of British helplessness, shot through with anti-Americanism, that gave birth to a policy of 'managed decline'. It was, in Anthony Nutting's summary of the FCO world view – in the title of his eponymous book on Suez – no end of a lesson; and it has infused the self-hating conventional wisdom of the political class to this day, and especially the Foreign Office, with a self-reinforcing enthusiasm for joining a neighbouring club which seemed, at that time, to be in their eyes not only more thriving but somehow more legitimately so. The moral dimension of this belief never was true and the economic one long since ceased to be.

But this declinist dogma estranged that class from ordinary folk who did not see their country that way at all but were unable to say so with any consequence until given the opportunity in June 2016. Therefore, adhesion could only be achieved in the 1970s by what Hugo Young described with deliberate *double entendre*, and approvingly, in his history of those years as 'this blessed plot' (Young 1998). Hence the deliberate deceit with which the decision to join the EEC was presented as merely an economic association by those who knew otherwise full well.

Argument two: The EU is in the zone of its own collapse

Stripped bare, the simple error which has permitted Treasury and Bank of England forecasts to be so gloomy and so wrong is that whereas they hypothesise many changes for Britain, they hold the state of the EU as more or less a constant. In fact, both parties are in dynamic change. Equally bluntly, being in harmony with leading trends for the 21st century world economy, Britain is thriving and can be even more if its Dysons and Bamfords and IT entrepreneurs and film-makers and research scientists and City folks are freed from excessive regulation and taxation; whereas the Eurozone is the world economy's most stubbornly stagnant region. But as I argued in a long essay published on the then new Briefings for Brexit website in April 2018, (Prins, 2018), the reasons for this are not conventionally economic. They are a consequence of the crisis of legitimacy that is shaking the EU to pieces.

When, in one of the most erudite and thoughtful books written about the experiment of European union, Larry Seidentop applied Alexis de Tocqueville's four tests of democracy from *Democracy in America* (1835-40) to the EU (Seidentop, 2000), he concluded, regretfully, that there was no culture of consent, nor likelihood of one emerging. He offered a darker warning too.

With a prescience that resonates 18 years later, he cautioned that, by allowing an elitist strategy for rapid European integration [the Monnet Method] to shape the image of liberal democracy in Europe, to the point almost of constituting it, Europe's centrist politicians may unwittingly be fostering the things that are most antithetical to liberal democracy: xenophobic nationalism and economic autarky. He concluded that these elites, of whom our grieving extreme Remainers are part, are putting the liberal democratic consensus at risk by opting for a policy of over-rapid integration.

As a thought experiment I applied a famous theory of the collapse of complex societies which in turn borrowed the concept of declining marginal return from investment managers, to the EU. The diagram summarises my findings.

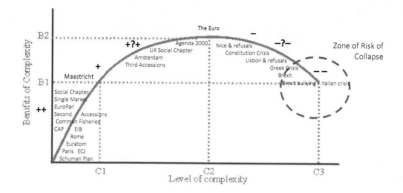

As Martin Selmayr, who took command of the Commission as its' chief bureaucrat in an administrative *coup d'etat* in spring 2018, struggles to keep his crumbling empire together it is therefore no wonder that he wishes Britain harm to discourage other potential escapees. All of which confirms the 'wisdom of unlettered men' in Edmund Burke's ringing phrase: those whom David Goodhart describes in his justly celebrated book (Goodhart, 2017) as the people from 'Somewhere': the 17.4m majority.

Argument three: Brexit is essential to protect British democracy and national security

From the moment of the decision to leave, the grieving losers have not accepted the result for a moment. And so we have a shocking moral and constitutional reason why the People's Vote of June 2016 must be obeyed by the political establishment. The venom of the extreme Remainer losers threatens the very life of our democracy. It must be drawn. Matthew Parris may hanker for a pre-lapsarian, pre-referendum politics: but Parliament willed it and it happened; and so his naughty analogy to capital punishment does not hold. (Parris, Matthew, 2018)

Writing as we approach the moment of departure, the 'extreme Remainers'' strategy of Brexit In Name Only '(Brexino') is finally clear in the detail of the Withdrawal Agreement (WA), in its annexes notably on the Irish backstop and in the pandemonium of devilish details surrounding them.

Astonishing alliances in defence of our democracy and security have emerged. On 24 November 2018, the legal verdict was in from Martin Howe QC: not just bad but atrocious. (Howe, 2018: 28-29). Then, on 29 November, the WA was condemned in terms and by people not seen criticising any Prime Minister so harshly since May 1940 (Dearlove et al, 2018).

For the first time in its history, Parliament is being asked to suspend its own sovereignty: it has no constitutional or moral right to do this. Any legislator that votes for it will not be forgiven. The 'deal' surrenders British national security by subordinating UK defence forces to Military EU control and compromising UK Intelligence capabilities. It puts at risk the fundamental Anglosphere alliances, specifically the vital Five Eyes Alliance and thereby threatens western security.

Number 10's livid and incompetent response was to single out a former Chief of MI6 and a Falklands Commander for reprimand: the first time a 'C' has been so castigated. But Sir Richard Dearlove and General Julian Thompson responded with a complete demolition of No 10's 'rebuttal' (Dearlove & Thompson, 2018). They documented how the May government is conspiring to surrender the 'crown jewels' of our national security, with British officials acting in collusion with the EC. The two subsequently wrote to MPs to advise and warn them to throw out the WA. Also without precedent.

The WA being much *worse* than membership, the only way to exit now is (as it always was) without negotiation, on World Trade Organisation rules. So the Extreme Remainers seek to demonise the way that we deal with most of the world for most of our trade and to pretend that we are unprepared to 'crash out' and so must accept vassalage.

Therefore, the courageous decision of an anonymous civil servant to contradict this lie in detail on 28 December 2018 – for the country is fully capable of leaving cleanly, without ransom payments – is both a sign of the advancing implosion of the May government and a good point at which to end. (Anonymous, 2018).

Not quite. The patriotic 17.4m have one other debt of thanks. It is to Ms Gina Miller and her Extreme Remainer colleagues whose success in the Supreme Court inscribed the date that we take back control into statute law, thereby ensuring that we do indeed leave on 29 March 2019 – and on

WTO terms without ransom. The exact opposite of what they intended. Fortunately, there are risks in being too clever by half!

Notes

1. For a fuller explanation of this and other parts of this chapter, see Prins, Gwythian (2016) "Beyond the Ghosts: does EU membership nourish or consume Britain's interests and global influence?", Minford, Patrick & Shackleton, J.R (eds), *Breaking Up is Hard to Do*, London: IEA, pp 58-79

References

Anonymous, (2018) " The Civil Service is ready for a no deal – but does the Government want you to think otherwise?" 28 December 2018, *The Daily Telegraph*, Available online at https://www.telegraph.co.uk/politics/2018/12/28/course-no-deal-has-planned-does-government-want-think-otherwise/

Dearlove, Sir Richard, et al, (2018) "A Message to the Prime Minister," 29 November 2018, *Briefings for Brexit,* Available online at https://briefingsforbrexit.com/a-message-to-the-prime-minister

Dearlove, Sir Richard & Thompson, General Julian, (2018) "The Prime Minister is misleading the country on defence and security – A rebuttal of a Downing Street 'reprimand,'" 5 December 2018, *Briefings for Brexit*, Available online at https://briefingsforbrexit.com/prime-minister-misleading-country-on-security/

Leach, R, (2004) *Europe: A Concise Encyclopaedia of the European Union*, Profile, London, 4th Edition

Howe, M (2018), "May's deal: a legal verdict", 24 November 2018, *The Spectator,*

Parris, Matthew (2018), "Why I don't, never have, and never will trust the people," 15 December 2018, *The Spectator.* Available online at https://www.spectator.co.uk/2018/12/why-i-dont-never-have-and-never-will-trust-the-people/#

Prins, G, (2018) *The EU is at clear risk of collapse and the remainiacs just don't see it* Available online at https://briefingsforbrexit.com/the-eu-is-at-clear-risk-of-collapse-and-the-remainiacs-just-dont-see-it/

Seidentop, L, (2000), *Democracy in Europe*, Penguin, Harmondsworth,

Ward AW & Gooch GP, (1923) *Cambridge History of British Foreign Policy, Vol II (1815-1866),* Cambridge University Press, Cambridge

Young, H, (1999), *This Blessed Plot: Britain and Europe from Churchill to Blair,* Penguin, Harmondsworth

About the contributor

Professor Gwythian Prins is an historian specialising in geo-politics and security issues. He is the Emeritus Research Professor at the London School of Economics and a former university lecturer in politics and Fellow in History at Emmanuel College, Cambridge. He has also served in the UK Defence Research Agency, at Nato Headquarters and on the Strategy Advisory Panel of British Chiefs of the Defence Staff. He is currently Visiting Senior Academic Fellow at L'Ecole Spéciale Militaire St Cyr, is Academic Board Member of Veterans for Britain and on the Editorial Board of *Briefings for Brexit.*

The geography vs history condundrum

Alex De Ruyter

This book has brought together a group of prominent academics to provide their views on the 'case for Brexit'. As a number of contributors have highlighted, much of the discourse from the Remain camp (a camp which it should be stated contains the overwhelming preponderance of academic consensus) has sought to quantify the costs associated with Brexit.

As contributors such as David Paton and Graham Gudgin have suggested, some of the assumptions underpinning these models can be legitimately questioned. Our contributors have also highlighted that the EU is far from perfect and have raised concerns over its perceived accountability to the public.

As we approach 29 March and beyond, what this book has made starkly clear is that the UK has always been something of a 'one-foot-in-the-door' member of the EU club with opt-outs of a number of prominent areas, most notably the Euro.

Brexit, perhaps paradoxically, revisits this with the prospective notion of being on the outside but wanting the other foot in. That is, regardless of the desire to escape the EU's alleged bureaucracy and restore 'sovereignty', on a practical level the UK and EU by necessity will continue to have close economic, political and security ties. In other words, geography trumps history.

This has been – and will continue to be – evident through the reality of deeply embedded manufacturing supply chains, the desire for continued regulatory alignment in key sectors such as financial services, environment, food standards, aviation and digital services amongst many others.

We will continue to have common interests in facing external threats and challenges. What type of Brexit – if any – we end up with will do little to change this.

Other Bite-Sized Brexit Books Published or in Preparation

John Mair, Neil Fowler (Editors)

Do They Mean Us?

The Foreign Correspondents' View of Brexit

Written by a range of distinguished foreign journalists, the book explores the spectrum of foreign responses to Brexit, the negotiations, and the outcomes for the UK and its partners.

Alex De Ruyter, David Bailey, John Mair (Editors)

Keeping the Wheels on the Road

UK Auto Post Brexit

With just-in-time and huge logistics issues, this book, written by world automotive experts, delves into the outcomes that can be expected post-Brexit and explores the responses that are required.

John Mair, Paul Davies

Will the Tory Party Ever Be the Same?

With the Tory Party in turmoil, is this an historic moment for the Tory Party? Leading Tories, with contributions promised from Michael Heseltine, distinguished historians, including Richard Gaunt of Nottingham University, and renowned commentators will provide insights into the likely outcomes.

Bite-Sized Public Affairs Books are designed to provide insights and stimulating ideas that affect us all in, for example, journalism, social policy, education, government and politics.

They are deliberately short, easy to read, and authoritative books written by people who are either on the front line or who are informed observers. They are designed to stimulate discussion, thought and innovation in all areas of public affairs. They are all firmly based on personal experience and direct involvement and engagement.

The most successful people all share an ability to focus on what really matters, keeping things simple and understandable. When we are faced with a new challenge most of us need quick guidance on what matters most, from people who have been there before and who can show us where to start. As Stephen Covey famously said, "The main thing is to keep the main thing, the main thing."

But what exactly is the main thing?

Bite-Sized books were conceived to help answer precisely that question crisply and quickly and, of course, be engaging to read, written by people who are experienced and successful in their field.

The brief? Distil the 'main things' into a book that can be read by an intelligent non-expert comfortably in around 60 minutes. Make sure the book enables the reader with specific tools, ideas and plenty of examples drawn from real life. Be a virtual mentor.

We have avoided jargon – or explained it where we have used it as a shorthand – and made few assumptions about the reader, except that they are literate and numerate, involved in understanding social policy, and that they can adapt and use what we suggest to suit their own, individual purposes. Most of all the books are focused on understanding and exploiting the changes that we witness every day but which come at us in what seems an incoherent stream.

They can be read straight through at one easy sitting and then referred to as necessary – a trusted repository of hard-won experience.

Bite-Sized Books Catalogue

Business Books

Ian Benn
> Write to Win
>> How to Produce Winning Proposals and RFP Responses

Matthew T Brown
> Understand Your Organisation
>> An Introduction to Enterprise Architecture Modelling

David Cotton
> Rethinking Leadership
>> Collaborative Leadership for Millennials and Beyond

Richard Cribb
> IT Outsourcing: 11 Short Steps to Success
>> An Insider's View

Phil Davies
> How to Survive and Thrive as a Project Manager
>> The Guide for Successful Project Managers

Paul Davies
> Developing a Business Case
>> Making a Persuasive Argument out of Your Numbers

Paul Davies
> Developing a Business Plan
>> Making a Persuasive Plan for Your Business

Paul Davies
> Contract Management for Non-Specialists

Paul Davies
> Developing Personal Effectiveness in Business

Paul Davies
> A More Effective Sales Team
>> Sales Management Focused on Sales People

Maiqi Ma
>Win with China
>>Acclimatisation for Mutual Success Doing Business with China

Elena Mihajloska
>Bridging the Virtual Gap
>>Building Unity and Trust in Remote Teams

Rob Morley
>Agile in Business
>>A Guide for Company Leadership

Gillian Perry
>Managing the People Side of Change
>>Ten Short Steps to Success in IT Outsourcing

Saibal Sen
>Next Generation Service Management
>>An Analytics Driven Approach

Don Sharp
>Nothing Happens Until You Sell Something
>>A Personal View of Selling Techniques

Christopher Hosford
>Great Business Meetings! Greater Business Results
>>Transforming Boring Time-Wasters into Dynamic Productivity Engines

Lifestyle Books

Anna Corthout
>Alive Again
>>My Journey to Recovery

Phil Davies
>Don't Worry Be Happy
>>A Personal Journey

Phil Davies
>Feel the Fear and Pack Anyway
>>Around the World in 284 Days

Stuart Haining
>My Other Car is an Aston
>>A Practical Guide to Ownership and Other Excuses to Quit Work and Start a Business

Bill Heine
Cancer – Living Behind Enemy Lines Without a Map
Regina Kerschbaumer
Yoga Coffee and a Glass of Wine
A Yoga Journey
Gillian Perry
Capturing the Celestial Lights
A Practical Guide to Imagining the Northern Lights
Arthur Worrell
A Grandfather's Story
Arthur Worrell's War

Public Affairs Books

Eben Black
Lies Lunch and Lobbying
PR, Public Affairs and Political Engagement – A Guide
John Mair and Richard Keeble (Editors)
Investigative Journalism Today:
Speaking Truth to Power
John Mair, Richard Keeble and Farrukh Dhondy (Editors)
V.S Naipaul:
The legacy
Christian Wolmar
Wolmar for London
Creating a Grassroots Campaign in a Digital Age
John Mair and Neil Fowler (Editors)
Do They Mean Us – Brexit Book 1
The Foreign Correspondents' View of the British Brexit

Fiction

Paul Davies
The Ways We Live Now
Civil Service Corruption, Wilful Blindness, Commercial Fraud, and Personal Greed – a Novel of Our Times
Paul Davies
Coming To
A Novel of Self-Realisation

Children's Books

Chris Reeve – illustrations by Mike Tingle
The Dictionary Boy
A Salutary Tale
Fredrik Payedar
The Spirit of Chaos
It Begins

Printed in Great Britain
by Amazon